D1648286

Giftbooks in this series by Helen Exley:

Words on Hope   Words on Joy
Words on Courage   Words on Kindness
Words of Wisdom   Words on Love and Caring

Published simultaneously in 1997 by Exley Publications in
Great Britain, and Exley Giftbooks in the USA.
Copyright © Helen Exley 1997
The moral right of the author has been asserted.

12 11 10 9 8 7 6

Edited and pictures selected by Helen Exley
ISBN 1-85015-919-X

Picture research by Image Select International.
Typeset by Delta, Watford.
Printed in China.

**Exley Publications Ltd, 16 Chalk Hill, Watford,
Herts WD19 4BG, UK.
Exley Publications LLC, 232 Madison Avenue,
Suite 1409, NY 10016, USA.**
www.helenexleygiftbooks.com

Words on Hope

A HELEN EXLEY
GIFTBOOK

EXLEY

NEW YORK • WATFORD, UK

*E*ACH SECOND

YOU CAN BE REBORN.

EACH SECOND

THERE CAN BE

A NEW BEGINNING.

IT IS CHOICE.

IT IS YOUR CHOICE.

CLEARWATER

A new life begins for us
with every second.
Let us go forward joyously
to meet it.
We must press on,
whether we will or no,
and we shall walk better
with our eyes before us
than with them
ever cast behind.

JEROME K. JEROME
(1859-1927)

NOW IS NO TIME TO THINK OF WHAT
YOU DO NOT HAVE.
THINK OF WHAT YOU CAN DO WITH
WHAT THERE IS.

ERNEST HEMINGWAY
(1899-1961)

*KEEP YOUR FACE
TO THE SUNSHINE
AND YOU CANNOT SEE
THE SHADOW.*

HELEN KELLER
(1880-1968)

Walk on a rainbow
trail; walk on a trail
of song,
and all about you
will be beauty.
There is a way out
of every dark mist,
over a rainbow trail.

NAVAJO SONG

THE FIRST SPARROW OF
SPRING! THE YEAR
BEGINNING WITH YOUNGER
HOPE THAN EVER!

HENRY DAVID THOREAU
(1817–1862)

Today

is the first day
of the rest
of your life.

DALE
CARNEGIE

People deal too much

with the negative,

and what is wrong....

Why not try and see

positive things,

to just touch those things

and make them bloom?

THICH NHAT HANH

*Hope is the thing
with feathers
That perches in the soul
And sings the tune
without the words,
And never stops at all
And sweetest in the gale
is heard.*

EMILY DICKINSON
(1830-1886)

*It seems to me we can never
give up longing and wishing
while we are thoroughly alive.
There are certain things
we feel to be beautiful and good,
and we <u>must</u> hunger
after them.*

GEORGE ELIOT
(MARY ANN EVANS)
(1819-1880)

*LIFE IS A PURE FLAME,

AND WE LIVE

BY AN INVISIBLE SUN

WITHIN US.*

SIR THOMAS BROWN
(1605-1682)

*Throw your heart
out in front of you
And run ahead
to catch it.*

ARAB PROVERB

When the heart weeps

for what it has lost,

the spirit laughs

for what it has found.

SUFI

APHORISM

I have always felt
that the moment when
first you wake up in the morning
is the most wonderful
of the twenty-four hours.
No matter how weary or dreary
you may feel, you
possess the certainty that...
absolutely anything
may happen. And the fact
that it practically always <u>doesn't</u>,
matters not one jot.
The possibility is always there.

MONICA BALDWIN

We have
enough people
who tell it
like it is —
now we could use
a few who tell it
like it can be.

ROBERT ORBEN

*There were many ways
of breaking a heart.
Stories were full of hearts
broken by love,
but what really broke
a heart
was taking away
its dream –
whatever that dream
might be.*

PEARL BUCK
(1892-1973)

When I look
into the future,
it's so bright it
burns my eyes.

OPRAH WINFREY, b. 1954

Hey,

this little kid gets roller skates.
She puts them on.
She stands up and almost
flops over backwards.
She sticks out a foot like
she's going somewhere and
falls down and
smacks her hand. She
grabs hold of a step to get up
and sticks out the other foot and
slides about six inches and
falls and skins her knee.
And then, you know what?
She brushes off the dirt and the

blood and puts some
spit on it and then
sticks out the other foot <u>again</u>.

MYRA COHN LIVINGSTON

If one burdens the future with one's worries, it cannot grow organically. I am filled with confidence, not that I shall succeed in worldly things, but that even when things go badly for me I shall still find life good and worth living.

ETTY HILLESUM

*But for me,
security is not knowing
what's going to happen.
Because if I don't know,
it could be terrific.*

GLORIA STEINEM, b. 1934

*If it were not for hopes,
the heart would break.*

THOMAS FULLER (1608-1661)

*THE HUMAN BODY
EXPERIENCES A POWERFUL
GRAVITATIONAL PULL IN THE
DIRECTION OF HOPE. THAT IS
WHY THE PATIENT'S HOPES*

ARE THE PHYSICIAN'S SECRET
WEAPON. THEY ARE THE
HIDDEN INGREDIENTS IN ANY
PRESCRIPTION.

NORMAN COUSINS

When you get into a
tight place and
everything goes
against you till it
seems as though you
could not hold on
a minute longer, never
give up then, for that
is just the place and
time that the tide
will turn.

HARRIET BEECHER STOWE
(1811–1896)

Then and there I invented this rule for myself to be applied to every decision I might have to make in the future. I would sort out all the arguments and see which belonged to fear and which to creativeness, and other things being equal I would make the decision which had the larger number of creative reasons on its side. I think it must be a rule something like this that makes jonquils and crocuses come pushing through the cold mud.

KATHARINE BUTLER HATHAWAY

*The longing
for paradise is paradise
itself.*

KAHLIL GIBRAN
(1 8 8 3 - 1 9 3 1)

*Hope
is the poor man's
bread.*

GEORGE HERBERT
(1 5 9 3 - 1 6 3 3)

I compared notes
with one of my friends
who expects everything
of the universe,
and is disappointed
when anything
is less than the best,
and I found that I begin
at the other extreme,
expecting nothing,
and am always
full of thanks
for moderate goods.

RALPH
WALDO
EMERSON
(1803-1882)

*O*ne of the best safeguards
of our hopes, I have suggested,
is to be able to mark off
the areas of hopelessness
and to acknowledge them,
to face them directly,
not with despair but with
the creative intent of
keeping them from polluting
all the areas
of possibility.

WILLIAM F. LYNCH

*Great hopes
make great people.*

THOMAS FULLER
(1608–1661)

I am not a has-been.
I'm a will be.

LAUREN BACALL,
b.1924

Grant me, O God,
the power to see
In every rose, eternity;
In every bud,
the coming day;
In every snow,
the promised May;
In every storm
the legacy
Of rainbows
smiling down at me!

VIRGINIA WUERFEL

For everyone who asks receives; he who seeks finds; and to him who knocks, the door will be opened.

MATTHEW 7:8

*I saw a delicate flower had
grown up two feet high, between
the horse's path and the wheel-
track. An inch more to the right
or left had sealed its fate, or an
inch higher; and yet it lived to
flourish as much as if it had
a thousand acres of untrodden
space around it, and never knew
the danger it occurred.
It did not borrow trouble,
nor invite an evil fate
by apprehending it.*

HENRY DAVID THOREAU
(1817-1862)

To love

is to risk not being loved

in return. To hope

is to risk disappointment.

But risks must be taken because

the greatest risk

in life is to risk nothing.

The person

who risks nothing,

does nothing,

sees nothing, has nothing

and is nothing.

He cannot learn,

feel, change, grow,

love and live.

AUTHOR UNKNOWN

TWO MEN LOOKED OUT OF
THE PRISON BARS;
THE ONE SAW MUD; THE OTHER
SAW STARS.

FREDERICK
LANGBRIDGE

THE UNENDURABLE

IS THE BEGINNING OF

THE CURVE OF JOY.

DJUNA BARNES
(1892-1982)

*May you
never miss
a rainbow
or a sunset
because you are
looking down.*

FROM
"SHARE THE HOPE"

Like all people who have nothing, I lived on dreams.

ANZIA YEZIERSKA

I believe in the sun,
even when it is not shining.
I believe in love,
even when I do not feel it.
I believe in God,
even when He is silent.

*No pessimist
ever discovered the secrets
of the stars,
or sailed to an
uncharted land, or opened
a new heaven to
the human spirit.*

HELEN KELLER
(1880-1968)

*There never was night
that had no morn.*

DINAH MULOCK CRAIK
(1826–1887)

When we can't dream any longer, we die.

EMMA GOLDMAN
(1869-1940)

Do not fear to hope...

Each time we smell the

autumn's dying scent,

We know that primrose time

will come again.

SAMUEL TAYLOR COLERIDGE
(1772-1834)

I avoid looking forward or

backward, and try to keep

looking upward.

CHARLOTTE BRONTE
(1816-1855)

*Even if I knew
that tomorrow
the world
would go to pieces,
I would still plant
my apple tree.*

MARTIN LUTHER
(1483–1546)

$\mathcal{T}$he old happiness
is withered and dead.
But, see, there is
a greenness veiling
the land...
the frail beginnings
of a new
and better life.

PAM BROWN, b.1928

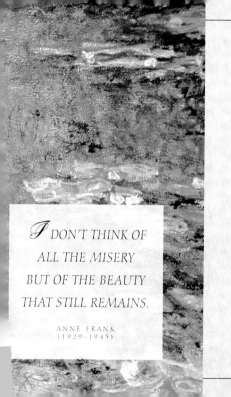

I DON'T THINK OF
ALL THE MISERY
BUT OF THE BEAUTY
THAT STILL REMAINS.

ANNE FRANK
(1929-1945)